Williamson  Publishing

Where kids READ for the REAL world!™

Make Your Own

BIRD-
HOUSES & FEEDERS

Robyn Haus

Illustrations by STAN JASKIEL

Quick Starts for Kids!™

WILLIAMSON PUBLISHING • CHARLOTTE, VERMONT

Library of Congress Cataloging-in-Publication Data

Haus, Robyn.
    Make your own birdhouses & feeders / Robyn Haus.
       p. cm. — (A Williamson quick starts for kids! book)
    Includes index.
    ISBN 1-885593-55-4 (pbk.)
    1. Birdhouses—Design and construction—Juvenile literature. 2. Bird feeders—Design and construction—Juvenile literature. [1. Birdhouses—Design and construction. 2. Bird feeders—Design and construction.] I. Title: Make your own birdhouses and feeders. II. Title. III. Series.

QL676.5 .H34 2001
690'.8927—dc21

2001025837

Quick Starts for Kids!™ series editor: **Susan Williamson**
Project editor: **Emily Stetson**
Interior design: **Linda Williamson, Dawson Design**
Interior illustrations: **Stan Jaskiel**
Cover design: **Marie Ferrante-Doyle**
Cover illustrations: **Michael Kline**
Cover photography: **David A. Seaver**
Printing: **Capital City Press**

Permission to use the following information is granted by Williamson Publishing Company from *Bird Tales from Near & Far* by Susan Milord, pages 20, 42–43, 58, 60–61; *Boredom Busters!* by Avery Hart and Paul Mantell, pages 27, 29–31; *Eco-Art!* by Laurie Carlson, pages 54–55, 64–65, 80; *The Kids' Nature Book* by Susan Milord, pages 32, 98–99, 123; and *The Little Hands Nature Book* by Nancy Castaldo, pages 128, 129.

Williamson Publishing Co.
P.O. Box 185
Charlotte, VT 05445
(800) 234-8791
Manufactured in the United States of America

10 9 8 7 6 5 4 3 2

Little Hands®, *Kids Can!*®, *Tales Alive!*®, and *Kaleidoscope Kids*® are registered trademarks of Williamson Publishing.

Good Times™, *Quick Starts for Kids!*™, *Quick Starts Tips!*™, *Quick Starts Jump-Starts*™, and *Where kids READ for the REAL World!*™ are trademarks of Williamson Publishing.

ROBYN HAUS is a bird-lover, parent, writer, and teacher who grew up bird-watching in the busy suburbs and now lives in Vermont's rural countryside.

CONTENTS

Tweedledum, Tweedledee & YOU!

You can almost set your seasonal watch to the birds, from the first birds of spring to the V-shaped formations of ducks and geese flying south in the fall. They cheer us up, make us laugh, bring us joy, and add color and music to our lives. But what do we do for them?

That's where you come in! A bird's life seems very good after a summer's gentle rain when the worms come out and your neighborhood is filled with chirping (that sounds like an international chorus of happy songs in many different languages). But it isn't always easy being a bird. Harsh winter weather, long periods of drought, destruction of both the natural habitat and the natural food chain, all make a bird's life, well — for the birds!

A Little Help from Their Friends!

Birds generally need just a little help from friends like you. To survive and be quite content, birds need these three things:

 FOOD: Even the simplest feeder or a bite of your pb&j sandwich can make a bird's life much easier. All that wing flapping burns lots of energy!

 SHELTER: Just a little place to call home — safe from predators like the neighborhood cat and comfy and safe for baby birds in the spring. If it could be out of the wind and rain, that would be very nice, indeed. Unravel that ratty old sweater and leave the yarn on a shrub; you'll be helping some birds build the perfect home.

 WATER: During a dry spell or a deep freeze, just set out a shallow bowl of water (even a Frisbee topped off with water works) for drinking and summertime bathing. Ah, so refreshing! In winter, break up the ice and add a few rocks so birds can drink without getting their feathers wet.

And that's just about it! You see, birds are just like you and me in what they need. Nothing fancy; just the basics.

Counting the Birds

Wherever you live, birds are on the move! Each spring and fall, one of the most amazing mysteries of nature begins: bird migration. In the fall, more than 350 species of birds leave for Mexico, Central and South America, and the Caribbean, traveling thousands of miles to their winter homes. These birds have a long flight before them. Some fly as far south as Argentina! Then, in late winter and early spring, the migrants begin their return.

And many of them may be flying right past your window or through your backyard. You can work with kids across the country to keep track of the birds you see by joining one of the national bird counts listed below.

**The Christmas Bird Count
is a one-day bird count**
in December. About 10 years ago Frank Chapman asked everybody to start a new holiday tradition — counting the birds! Only 27 bird-lovers responded. Now, tens of thousands of people tally wrens, grackles, doves, and lots of other species all over the Americas. Want to join in? Find out how at
<www.birdsource.org/cbc/involved.htm>
or write to Christmas Bird Count,
National Audubon Society,
700 Broadway, New York, NY 10003.

The Great Backyard Bird Count is a four-day count of bird populations across North, Central, and South America in late winter. Nothing could be simpler. Your count can be taken anywhere you happen to be during the four days in the middle of February. You report it online; no preregistration required. Your data helps researchers find out where the birds are, how the winter weather has influenced bird populations, and if birds are wintering as far north or south as they were in past years. Every count is important, whether you see five birds or 75! To find out more, check out the GBBC website at <**http:birdsource.cornell.edu/gbbc/**> or contact the National Audubon Society (see page 5 for address).

Project FeederWatch is a winter-long bird count of birds that visit feeders from November to April throughout North America. Anyone — kids, classrooms, families, youth groups, and individuals — can join in. You set up bird-count days every two weeks, and report your findings to the researchers at the Cornell Lab of Ornithology, who use your data to track how bird populations change throughout the winter season. You provide a feeder and seed. To register for the count online, contact <**http:birds.cornell.edu/pfw/**> or write: Project FeederWatch, Cornell Lab of Ornithology, 159 Sapsucker Woods Road, Ithaca, NY 14850.

Thanks for making your interest in nature count! Now, if you want to find out how to care for the birds in your neighborhood — and how to attract a particular kind of bird that lives in your part of North America — then read on. It's a lot of fun, plus you'll be helping your feathered friends!

FAST FOOD!

The Quick Starts™ Guide to Bird Feeding

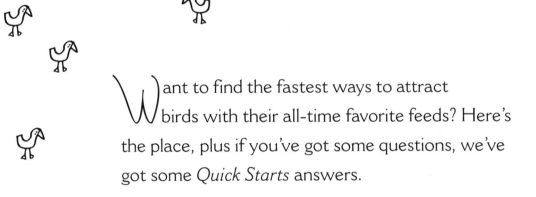

Want to find the fastest ways to attract birds with their all-time favorite feeds? Here's the place, plus if you've got some questions, we've got some *Quick Starts* answers.

When's the best time to start feeding birds?

Anytime is good, but in northern areas, try to begin in early fall, so the birds will find your feeder before cold weather sets in. Fall feeding also helps young birds that are learning to fend for themselves and gives a boost to migratory birds that need to put on fat before they begin their long flight south.

Should I feed the birds in the summer, too, or will that just make them lazy and dependent?

Good question! There's lots of confusion about year-round feeding. The birds need your help the most in winter, no doubt about that. And in the early spring while they are building nests and laying their eggs, an easy meal would be most appreciated. After that, it's up to you. If you want to attract different types of birds all year, then you will need to feed them. Otherwise, the birds can do fine in spring and summer on their own, unless there is a serious drought.

Will birds die if I stop feeding them?

If that worry is preventing you from feeding the birds, then get started now! Birds forage for food in the wild quite naturally. If your feeder goes empty, the birds will simply search harder for their supper elsewhere. A sudden lack of food — especially in snowy or freezing weather — might be hard on them, though, just as it would be for you! So if you are going away, ask a friend to keep your birds' tummies full. And try to keep feeding them until early spring!

Buying bird feed isn't in our budget, but I really want a feeder. What can I do?

Good news! Birds like a lot of the same food that you do, so some table scraps will fill the bill. (Get it?) Offer some stale bread, popped popcorn, peanut butter, chopped nuts, corn, raisins, fruit, and cereal. Just set the food out where it will stay dry or combine it into easy-to-make bird-pleasing recipes (see pages 14–19). And don't forget all the berries and nuts that you can collect and dry in summer and serve in winter — free for the taking!

Do birds choke on peanut butter?

No, not that we know. But you can make peanut butter easier for the birds to swallow if you mix it with grit, cornmeal, or suet to break up the stickiness (see pages 17–19 for recipes).

How can I attract some different kinds of birds to my feeder?

Just like you, birds have likes and dislikes when it comes to food and feeders. Offering a variety of foods in several different kinds of feeders will appeal to more types of birds (especially small birds that get pushed aside by the larger ones). For more on which feeders and foods to use for which birds, see pages 58–59.

I'm discouraged. Squirrels are eating all the food I put out!

They're at it again! Well, don't let squirrels baffle you — put up a baffle to stop them! See pages 33–34 for tips on how to squirrel-proof a feeder. Or, offer the squirrels their own feeding station (see page 34).

We have a cat. Can I still feed the birds?

Well, I won't kid you, cats are a serious threat to birds (and the idea is to feed the birds, not turn them into cat food)! The best option is to keep your cat indoors, so the birds will be safe. For more tips on protecting the birds, see page 46.

Extra-easy feeding

• *Numero uno!* Just getting started feeding the birds? Try black-oil sunflower seed first! Most birds love it. Then, try other seeds or mixtures.

• *Cheap, cheap, cheap!* A good way to get a bargain on high-quality birdseed is to buy the kinds you need in bulk from feed-and-seed and some hardware stores and mix it yourself to guarantee you aren't paying for any filler.

Birds' All-Time Favorite Feeds!

You know what it's like to be faced with a dinner that you can hardly look at, much less eat. Well, birds are a lot like you: They have food preferences. Some birds are seedeaters (like quails and doves), others are insect eaters (woodpeckers, cardinals, and finches), and some prefer to sip nectar or eat fruit (tanagers and hummingbirds). Then there are birds — like starlings — who eat practically anything, so it's hard to keep them from hogging the feast!

Also like we humans, birds tend to favor and need certain kinds of foods at different times of year — just as we might choose hot cocoa in the winter and icy lemonade in the summer! They need chopped nuts and suet — a kind of high-fat food that helps them keep warm — in winter, along with some grit to help them digest it. In late spring, sweeter, softer foods are welcome as they begin to feed their babies.

Here are the top food choices of birds across North America. You're sure to have dinner guests if you offer a sampling of these favorites!

Black-oil sunflower seed. This is the hands-down favorite — some experts call it the "hamburger of the bird world"! These small, thin-shelled seeds are easy for small birds to handle and crack, and the inside offers lots of the high-fat, high-energy food birds need in winter. Yumm!

Suet. This is just a fancy name for white beef fat that you can get at the meat counter at the supermarket. It's a terrific source of energy for winter birds. Nuthatches and woodpeckers will gobble it up! (See pages 16–18 for ways to serve it.)

Peanuts. Put out chopped unroasted and unsalted raw peanuts for easiest feasting, and you'll be very popular with woodpeckers, jays, nuthatches, chickadees, and titmice.

Cracked corn. There's sure to be lots of activity at your feeder, as sparrows, blackbirds, jays, doves, quails, *and* squirrels all like cracked corn.

Safflower seed. Supposedly northern cardinals and many other birds like this a lot, and squirrels and blackbirds don't really favor it. Try it and see!

Niger/thistle seed. Finches and other small birds love these, so serve thistle seed in a tube feeder with small holes (to keep bigger-beaked birds away!) or in a sock-shaped, fine-mesh "thistle sock."

Mixed seed. Good mixed seed has a lot of sunflower seed, cracked corn, millet, and perhaps some peanut hearts in it. Avoid seed mixes with lots of "filler" such as wheat — many birds just scratch it aside. (Hmmm! Sound familiar?)

Fruit. Tanagers and orioles will flock to a fruit buffet in spring and summer, but many winter birds also like fruit. Set out grapes, sliced citrus fruits, apples, or bananas, and even melon rinds. If you want to feed them raisins, first chop them up and soften them in warm water.

Mealworms. Don't say "Yuck!" before you try out these beetle larvae on the birds! They're favorites of insect eaters, such as woodpeckers and robins, especially in winter when fresh food is in short supply. You can buy mealworms in bait and pet stores. Once you have them, you can raise more of your own (see this page)!

Sugar water. This warm-weather hummingbird food might be just what your "hummers" need during the winter months, if you live in parts of Texas or the Gulf states. In the North, hummingbirds will appreciate a nectar-rich resting stop in the fall, to refuel on their trek south (see recipe, page 15).

Start a Mealworm Nursery!

Raising mealworms is easy – and fun! Choose any container with a lid, such as an old shoebox, a jar, or an oatmeal container. Stock it about half full with cornmeal, bran, dry oatmeal, or cracker crumbs. Add a few fruit or potato slices on top. Drop the mealworm larvae (available at pet or bait stores) into the nursery and cover the container with cheesecloth or a plastic lid with tiny holes pricked through it (anything that allows air to get in but won't let the larvae escape). Feed a serving of mealworms in a small bowl (so the worms won't escape) to the birds. Add more cornmeal or bran every couple of months to keep your mealworm meals going.

Matching the Birds to Their Feeds to ... YOU!

The only things you need to know to feed the birds before using the handy Mix-'n'-Match! chart on pages 58–59 are where you live (duh!), the birds you hope to attract (look in a field guide to the birds or on the web at <**http://birdsource.cornell.edu/gbbcguideframes.html**> for your area of the country to see who's who), where to buy good feed inexpensively, and how to make the type of feeder you'll need (see pages 20–34). Then, you'll be ready to feed the birds!

Quick Starts Jump-Starts™

Feeder Frenzy

Don't know where to start? Try some of the easy-to-make feeders on page 21, filled with sunflower seeds, fruit, and other bird-food favorites from the list on pages 10–11. Easier yet? Fill a yogurt cup or tuna-fish can with dry cereal, breadcrumbs, or popped popcorn mixed with a little peanut butter. Hang it from a tree or place it on a bench or tree stump. Then, just sit back and watch!

Eat Like a Bird

If you've ever been told that you eat like a bird, maybe you better slow it up a bit! Although many people think that birds eat very little, the truth is, most birds eat the equivalent of one-quarter of their weight in food each day! (That means if you weigh 60 pounds/27 kg, you'd eat 15 pounds/7 kg of food each day in birdland!)

And migrating birds really pack it on: Some increase their weight by as much as 50 percent (gaining half of what they already weigh) before they begin their journey!

Bet you're glad you don't *really* eat like a bird!

CRUNCHIES

Make Your Own Birdhouses & Feeders

COME 'N' GET IT!

Recipes for a Homemade Feast

Feeding the birds is easy, especially when you use fixings you already have on hand. Make a batch of your own feed, using ingredients most favored by the birds you want to attract (see Mix-'n'-Match!, pages 58–59).

Do-It-Yourself Mixes

You won't be disappointed — and the birds won't be either — if you start with a favorite, such as black-oil sunflower seed and cracked corn. For more variety, add millet, canary seed, and chopped nuts. Don't forget to toss in some leftovers, too! Experiment to get the best mix for your birds. You'll quickly learn what they eat … and what they leave behind for you to clean up!

Quick Starts Tips!™

Part of the mix

All of the amounts in the mixes are approximate, so you don't have to measure precisely. And the term "part" simply means a ratio or relationship: 1 part to 2 parts would mean 1 cup or yogurt container or whatever to 2 cups or yogurt containers or whatever.

Crowd Pleaser

1 part black-oil sunflower seed
1 part cracked corn

Mix and serve in feeders.

Health Mix

3 parts black-oil sunflower seed
3 parts white proso millet
1 part finely cracked corn
Grit, 1 teaspoon (5 ml) per quart of seed

Mix and serve in feeders.

"Chirp! They're serving leftovers at the Smiths's house today!"

Quick Starts Tips!™

No birdseed available? Serve some leftovers instead! Popped popcorn, cereal or granola, raisins, stale bread, cooked potatoes, piecrust, and cake, cookie, and cracker crumbs are all welcome bird foods. (The grape jelly from your pb&j is an oriole favorite!)

Hummingbird Nectar

Serve up a sweet drink for the hummers, orioles, and tanagers in the feeder on page 32. Cardinals, woodpeckers, finches, and thrushes might stop by for a sip as well!

$1/4$ cup (50 ml) sugar
$1/4$ cup (50 ml), plus $3/4$ cup (175 ml) cold water

1. With adult help, heat the sugar and $1/4$ cup (50 ml) water in a heavy saucepan, stirring until the mixture comes to a boil.

2. Remove from the stove, and stir in $3/4$ cup (175 ml) cold water. Cool completely before filling the feeder. Extra sugar water can be stored in your refrigerator for up to a week.

Quick Starts Tips!™

Hummer hints

Follow these guidelines for the best nectar ever:

- Use only water and sugar solutions — never honey (it encourages a mold that can infect a hummingbird's tongue).
- Avoid adding red food coloring to sugar water — it's unnecessary and possibly harmful. A red ribbon or orange surveyor's tape tied on top of the feeder will attract hummers just as well.
- Empty the feeder and clean it with hot, soapy water every week.

Fine Fat Specialties

*B*ring out the fat! (For the birds, not for us humans, that is!) Suet and other fats are bird favorites in fall, winter, and spring, when birds need all the energy they can get. In winter, put out a chunk of suet (available from the meat department of your supermarket) or make your own suet treats by mixing suet or other fats with bird foods. Try suet substitutes, such as peanut butter and vegetable shortening, too.

Basic Suet Mixture

Collect some fat such as suet, lard, or the drippings from roasts and bacon, purchased seeds, bits of dried fruit, and whatever bird edibles you have on hand. Use roughly 1/2 pound (250 g) of fat for every pound (500 g) of dry ingredients. Melt or soften the fat (ask for adult help with this step); then add the dry ingredients, mixing well. Pour it into a container, chill to harden in your refrigerator, and serve it to the birds!

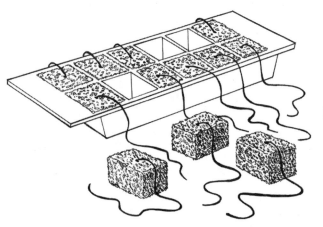

Super-Simple Seed Cubes

Melted suet or softened
vegetable shortening
Unroasted and unsalted peanut bits
Raisins or chopped apple
Birdseed
Ice-cube tray
String

1. Mix in the solid ingredients with the melted suet.
2. Pour the mixture into an ice-cube tray (ask for adult help with any hot liquids).
3. Insert a short piece of string into each cube.
4. Put the tray in your freezer to harden into easy-to-hang cubed bird treats!

Make Your Own Birdhouses & Feeders

Bird Bell

½ cup (125 ml) peanut butter

1 cup (250 ml) birdseed

2½ cups (625 ml) cornmeal

½ cup (125 ml) softened vegetable shortening
   or melted suet

Small yogurt container or paper cup

Cardboard circle, about 2" (5 cm) in diameter

Nail or sharp pencil, for poking hole

Yarn

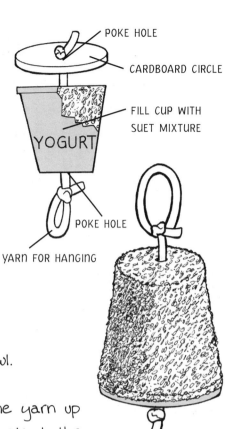

POKE HOLE

CARDBOARD CIRCLE

FILL CUP WITH SUET MIXTURE

YOGURT

POKE HOLE

YARN FOR HANGING

1. Mix the ingredients together in a large bowl.
2. Make the bell as shown.
3. Press the mixture into the cup and pull the yarn up tight so the cardboard circle fits snugly against the bottom.
4. Chill to harden; then cut or peel the cup away. Hang the birdseed bell from a tree so the flock can feast!

Bird Cupcakes: Drop the peanut butter-birdseed-fat mixture into the cups of greased muffin tins or paper muffin cups. Push a stick through the middle of each "cupcake" to create a hole for hanging. Chill to harden, remove sticks, and thread yarn through the hole (knot at one end) to hang.

Suet Cakes: To make your own suet cakes, use the BASIC SUET MIXTURE to fill muffin tins, tuna-fish or cat-food cans, yogurt or cottage cheese containers, coffee or soup cans — whatever you have on hand — chill to harden; then hang with yarn.

Sunflower Seed Log

Roll the Winter Breakfast mixture (see below) into a log shape, coat with sunflower seeds, and chill until solid. Hang with string or ribbon for easy feeding!

Winter Breakfast

1½ cups (375 ml) suet, chopped
½ cup (125 ml) peanut butter
¼ cup (50 ml) granulated sugar
1 cup (250 ml) cornmeal
½ cup (125 ml) cooked oatmeal
½ cup (125 ml) birdseed mixture, or more as needed

Mix the ingredients together, and spoon into a coffee-can feeder (page 23) or feeder stick (page 26).

True Grit

Since birds don't have teeth, they eat small, hard materials like sand and gravel to help them break up their food in their gizzards. You can purchase grit at pet stores or feed stores, or make your own. Add some grit to suet and peanut butter recipes to make them easier to eat. This simple grit recipe uses eggshells to help birds digest their food (and it provides much-needed calcium in early spring as well).

Bake rinsed eggshells for 20 minutes at 250°F (120°C). Crush them to smaller-than-a-dime size. Serve the eggshells in a dish or on a low platform feeder (page 27), separate from the seed. Or, mix with suet or peanut butter.

Make Your Own Birdhouses & Feeders

Summer Treat

Young birds and fruit-lovers like tanagers and orioles will appreciate the jelly in this mix!

5 parts cornmeal
1 part peanut butter
½ part softened vegetable shortening
½ part apple, grape, or currant jelly

Mix ingredients together. Spoon into tuna-fish cans or other feeders to serve.

Now that you have the menu planned, let's "build the restaurant" so the birds can eat in their preferred style!

BUILD A SONGBIRD CAFÉ!

Quick Starts™ Fun Feeders

When it comes to feeding birds, simpler is usually better! Bird feeders don't have to be expensive or complicated. If you match the feeder style (such as tray or hanging) and the feed to the needs of the birds in your area, you're bound to have success. And to give your Songbird Café a five-star rating, protect your bird friends from predators like the neighborhood cat and protect the feed from squirrels.

Favorite Easy-to-Make Feeders

Here are three of our favorite easy-to-make bird feeders. We like them because they are fun to make, they look very nice in a tree, and the birds seem to really like them, too! For more Quick Starts™ easy-to-make feeders, look on pages 22–23.

Grapevine Wreath Feeder

Shape a single length of vine into a circle (pull the leaves off first). Wrap more vines over and under this circle until you have a thick wreath. Use thin wire or twine to hold them together in a circular shape. Decorate the wreath with corncobs, sunflowers, chokecherries, fruit slices, nuts, cranberries, and other natural bird foods.

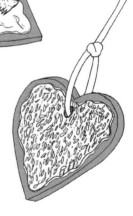

Cookie-Cutter Snacks

Cut shapes from stale bread, poke a hole with a drinking straw, and thread with string. Slather with peanut butter, jelly, and birdseed!

Winter Treat Garlands

String day-old bread, orange rounds (first cut into fourths), popped popcorn, and fresh cranberries onto about a yard (m) of heavy-duty thread, stringing the food in a pattern and leaving a few inches (cm) between foods.

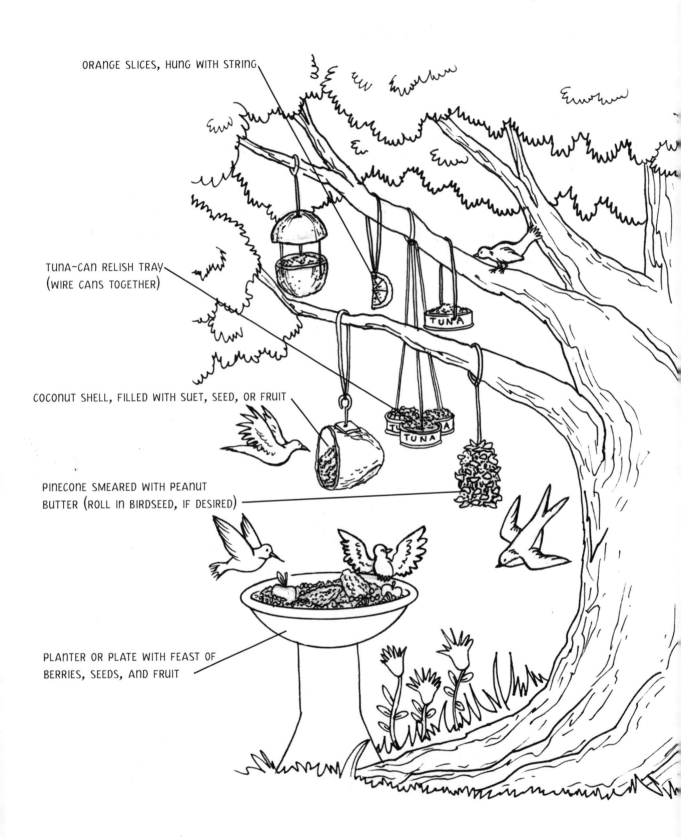

ORANGE SLICES, HUNG WITH STRING

TUNA-CAN RELISH TRAY
(WIRE CANS TOGETHER)

COCONUT SHELL, FILLED WITH SUET, SEED, OR FRUIT

PINECONE SMEARED WITH PEANUT
BUTTER (ROLL IN BIRDSEED, IF DESIRED)

PLANTER OR PLATE WITH FEAST OF
BERRIES, SEEDS, AND FRUIT

Make Your Own Birdhouses & Feeders

FEED THE BIRDS!

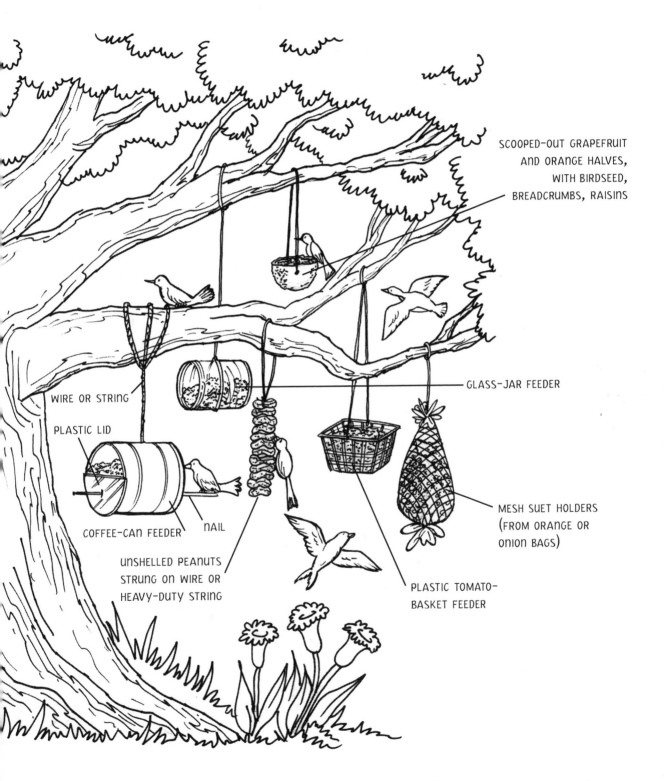

SCOOPED-OUT GRAPEFRUIT AND ORANGE HALVES, WITH BIRDSEED, BREADCRUMBS, RAISINS

WIRE OR STRING

PLASTIC LID

GLASS-JAR FEEDER

COFFEE-CAN FEEDER

NAIL

MESH SUET HOLDERS (FROM ORANGE OR ONION BAGS)

UNSHELLED PEANUTS STRUNG ON WIRE OR HEAVY-DUTY STRING

PLASTIC TOMATO-BASKET FEEDER

Build a Songbird Café!

Restaurant Rules & Regulations!

Every eating establishment has rules and regulations to safeguard the patrons and the neighbors. Here are the ones we hope you will follow:

- **Leftover Lane.** Birds may love your leftovers, but the neighbors probably won't be pleased if your café turns into a garbage pit. Need I say more?

- **Safe & Simple.** Avoid sharp edges that could injure birds, along with tight crevices that might trap their feet. And plan ahead: If a feeder is hard to reach, chances are it will sit empty most of the time.

- **Beware the Neighborhood Cat!** When looking for a "pounce-free" zone for your café, consider placing it away from dense shrubs that cats and critters can hide in. Place all tray and platform feeders several feet (m) away from brush piles and shrubbery.

- **Hold the (Dried) Coconut.** Fresh coconut (served in ready-to-eat coconut halves) is a welcome treat, but don't be tempted to add the shredded, dried kind to your bird buffet. Dried coconut may swell inside a bird's body.

- **Wash Your Hands.** After working with feeders and houses, be sure to wash your hands with soap and water. Birds carry germs just like any other critters.

Quick Starts Tips!™

Mornin', mourning doves!

Birds feed most during the morning hours, so hang some feeders where you can see them from the breakfast table!

Holidays Are for the Birds

• **Give a bird-treat gift!** Save tuna-fish tin cans, with just one end removed. Wrap the sides in colorful paper and tie with enough yarn to tie the feeder onto a tree branch. Slide a small stick under the bottom to be used as a perch for birds. Make the Basic Suet Mixture (see page 16) and fill the tins. Give as a gift to a bird-loving friend!

• **Trim a tree for the birds.** Decorate a tree in your yard with edible ornaments for the holiday season. Hang cookie-cutter feeders, winter treat garlands, scooped-out orange halve feeders, pretzels, gingerbread cookies – even peanut butter bagels!

• **Give a bird a valentine!** Don't forget your feathered friends on February 14 – or anytime! Make a cardboard valentine and "paint" it with suet or peanut butter. Sprinkle with seeds for an extra-special treat! Vary the seed varieties to attract different types of birds.

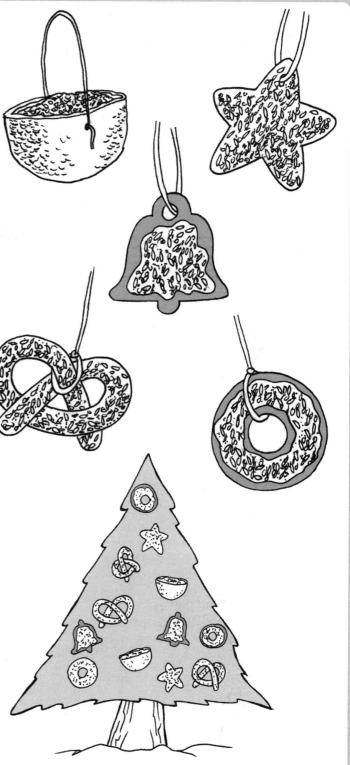

Eight Bird Feeders to Build

Once you've tried out the super-simple feeders, make your own Songbird Café. You'll want a variety of feeds and a variety of feeders. To get started, we suggest this assortment of feeders:

Super-Simple Feeder Stick (page 26)
Trusty Tray or Platform Feeder (page 27)
Tiny Spaces Window Feeder (page 29)
Five-Star Café (page 30)
Edible "Birdhouse" (page 31)
Wire-Mesh Tube Feeder (page 32)
Hummingbird Feeder (page 32)
Rockin' Robin Diner (page 33)

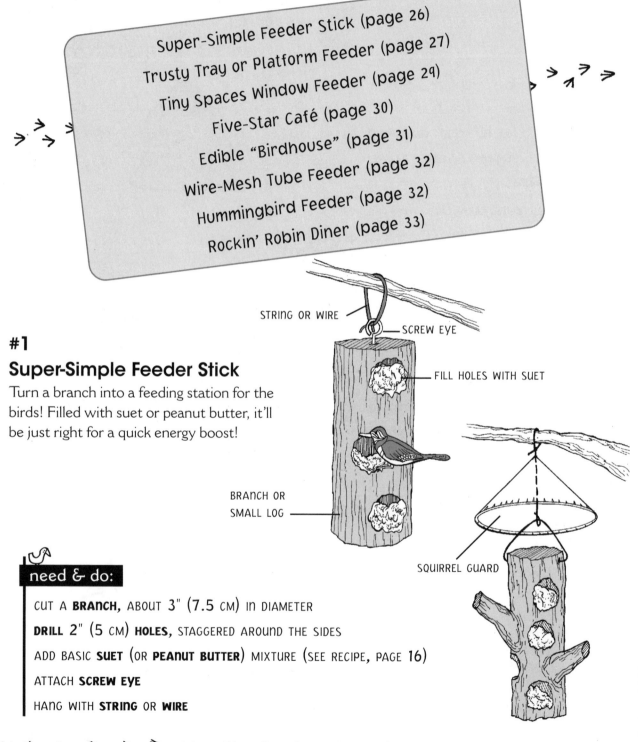

STRING OR WIRE
SCREW EYE
FILL HOLES WITH SUET
BRANCH OR SMALL LOG
SQUIRREL GUARD

#1

Super-Simple Feeder Stick

Turn a branch into a feeding station for the birds! Filled with suet or peanut butter, it'll be just right for a quick energy boost!

need & do:

CUT A **BRANCH**, ABOUT 3" (7.5 CM) IN DIAMETER

DRILL 2" (5 CM) **HOLES**, STAGGERED AROUND THE SIDES

ADD BASIC **SUET** (OR **PEANUT BUTTER**) MIXTURE (SEE RECIPE, PAGE 16)

ATTACH **SCREW EYE**

HANG WITH **STRING** OR **WIRE**

Make Your Own Birdhouses & Feeders

#2
Trusty Tray or Platform Feeder

Any flat, raised surface can serve as a tray or
platform feeder. Tray feeders are great because
they attract most species of feeder birds, and
the raised surface keeps the seed from
becoming soggy and spoiling on the
damp ground.

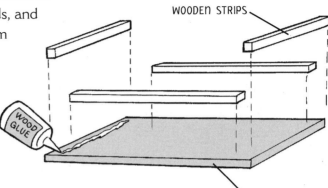

WOODEN STRIPS

WOOD GLUE

SCRAP WOOD

need & do:

WOODEN PLATFORM, ABOUT 10" x 20" (25 x 50 CM)

GLUE OR **NAIL STICKS** OR 1" (2.5 CM) **STRIPS OF WOOD** ALONG SIDES

ALLOW **GAPS** FOR DRAINAGE

FILL WITH **SEED** OR **FRUIT**

ADD **SCREW EYES** INTO CORNERS TO HANG **CHAIN** (OPTIONAL)

BIRDSEED

GAPS FOR DRAINAGE

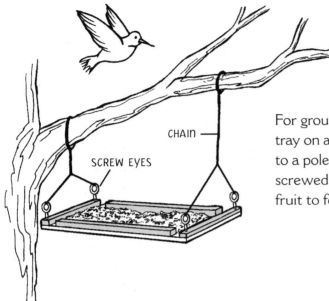

CHAIN

SCREW EYES

For ground feeders, like doves and jays, place the tray on a stump. To mount it higher, nail the platform to a pole. Or hang it from a tree branch with chains screwed into the corners. Put just enough seed or fruit to feed the birds for a day or so.

Keep It Neat!

You don't have to be a neatness nut when you feed the birds, but a little light housekeeping won't hurt. Birds can become sick from wet or moldy seeds or hulls and from accumulating bird droppings, so keep the tray clean.

Give the feeder a thorough cleaning at least once a season (more often if you live in a warmer climate). Scrub the platform surface with soap and water, and dip or rinse it with a weak bleach solution (1 part bleach – use only with adult help – to 9 parts water). Then, rinse and dry the feeder, refill it, and set it out again for more feasting!

Roof Out the Weather: For a fancier feeder that keeps off the snow and rain, nail a short piece of wood upright in each corner and add another 10" x 20" (25 x 50 cm) scrap of wood on top for a roof.

#3

Tiny Spaces Window Feeder

This homemade feeder can sit outside your window, providing a welcome "fill 'er up" spot for birds.

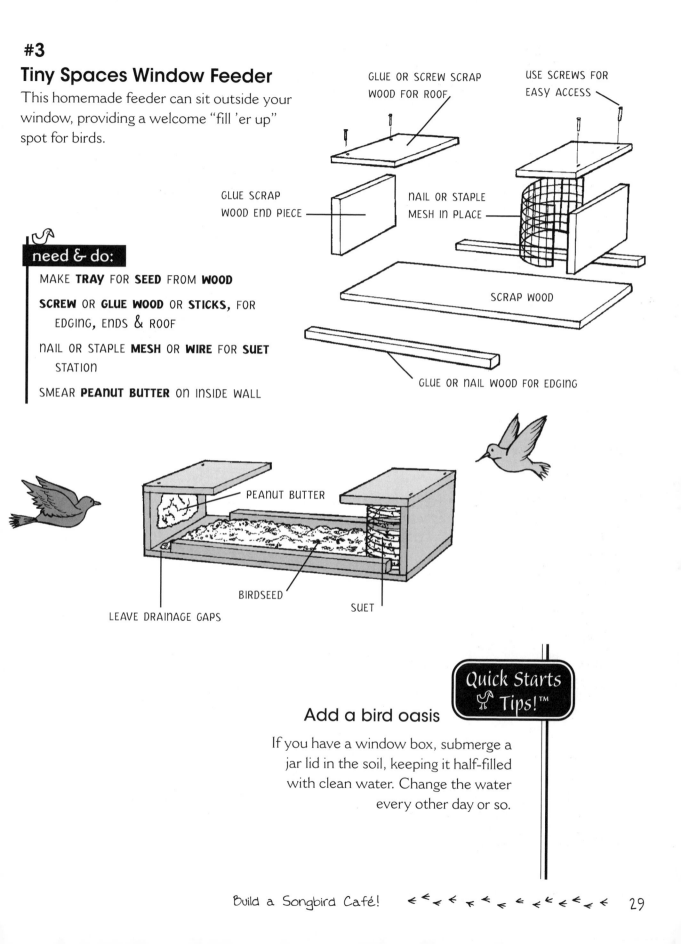

GLUE OR SCREW SCRAP WOOD FOR ROOF

USE SCREWS FOR EASY ACCESS

GLUE SCRAP WOOD END PIECE

NAIL OR STAPLE MESH IN PLACE

SCRAP WOOD

GLUE OR NAIL WOOD FOR EDGING

need & do:

MAKE **TRAY** FOR **SEED** FROM **WOOD**

SCREW OR **GLUE WOOD** OR **STICKS**, FOR EDGING, ENDS & ROOF

NAIL OR STAPLE **MESH** OR **WIRE** FOR **SUET** STATION

SMEAR **PEANUT BUTTER** ON INSIDE WALL

PEANUT BUTTER

BIRDSEED

SUET

LEAVE DRAINAGE GAPS

Quick Starts Tips!™

Add a bird oasis

If you have a window box, submerge a jar lid in the soil, keeping it half-filled with clean water. Change the water every other day or so.

#4

Five-Star Café *(with a Rain Shield)*

Give your bird café the ultimate in dining comfort by making a covered feeder with walls to keep out the rain, snow, and sleet!

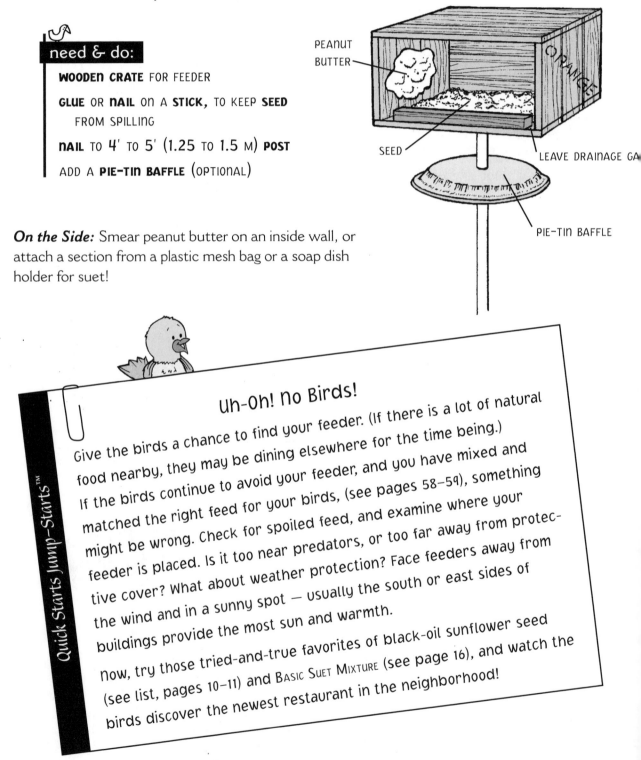

need & do:

WOODEN CRATE FOR FEEDER

GLUE OR **NAIL** ON A **STICK,** TO KEEP **SEED** FROM SPILLING

NAIL TO 4' TO 5' (1.25 TO 1.5 M) **POST**

ADD A **PIE-TIN BAFFLE** (OPTIONAL)

PEANUT BUTTER

SEED

LEAVE DRAINAGE GA[...]

PIE-TIN BAFFLE

On the Side: Smear peanut butter on an inside wall, or attach a section from a plastic mesh bag or a soap dish holder for suet!

Quick Starts Jump-Starts™

Uh-Oh! No Birds!

Give the birds a chance to find your feeder. (If there is a lot of natural food nearby, they may be dining elsewhere for the time being.) If the birds continue to avoid your feeder, and you have mixed and matched the right feed for your birds, (see pages 58–59), something might be wrong. Check for spoiled feed, and examine where your feeder is placed. Is it too near predators, or too far away from protective cover? What about weather protection? Face feeders away from the wind and in a sunny spot — usually the south or east sides of buildings provide the most sun and warmth.

Now, try those tried-and-true favorites of black-oil sunflower seed (see list, pages 10–11) and BASIC SUET MIXTURE (see page 16), and watch the birds discover the newest restaurant in the neighborhood!

#5
Edible "Birdhouse" *(with an Oat-Thatched Roof)!*

You can buy one of these quite expensive edible "birdhouses" (not a
house for living in, just for eating) — or you can make one, using
household items, that the birds will enjoy at least as much!
Because this version is made out of cardboard, it won't
really house any birds, but it's great for feasting!

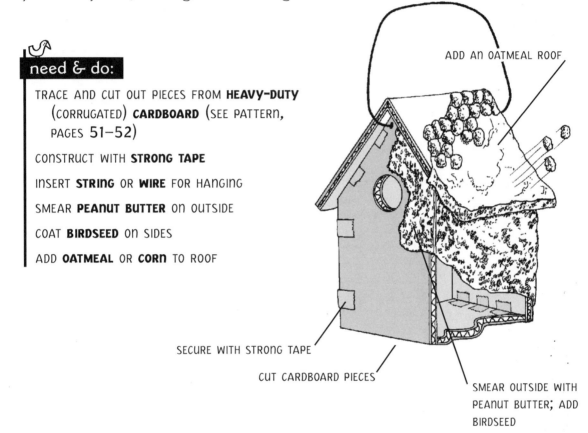

need & do:

TRACE AND CUT OUT PIECES FROM **HEAVY-DUTY**
   (CORRUGATED) **CARDBOARD** (SEE PATTERN,
   PAGES 51–52)

CONSTRUCT WITH **STRONG TAPE**

INSERT **STRING** OR **WIRE** FOR HANGING

SMEAR **PEANUT BUTTER** ON OUTSIDE

COAT **BIRDSEED** ON SIDES

ADD **OATMEAL** OR **CORN** TO ROOF

ADD AN OATMEAL ROOF

SECURE WITH STRONG TAPE

CUT CARDBOARD PIECES

SMEAR OUTSIDE WITH
PEANUT BUTTER; ADD
BIRDSEED

Milk-Carton "Birdhouse" Feeder: Use a half-gallon (2 L)
milk carton for the base, instead of the cardboard pattern,
adding a perch and hole.

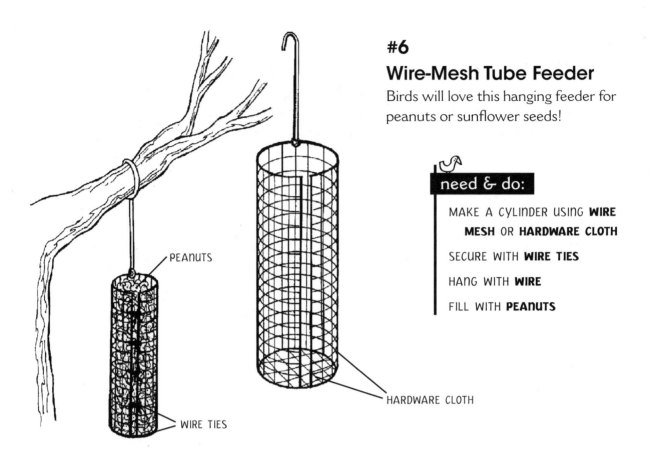

#6
Wire-Mesh Tube Feeder

Birds will love this hanging feeder for peanuts or sunflower seeds!

PEANUTS

WIRE TIES

HARDWARE CLOTH

need & do:

MAKE A CYLINDER USING **WIRE MESH** OR **HARDWARE CLOTH**

SECURE WITH **WIRE TIES**

HANG WITH **WIRE**

FILL WITH **PEANUTS**

#7
A Humdinger of a Feeder!

Entice some hummingbirds to dine at your café with this custom-designed feeder in their favorite color! (To decorate, magenta nail polish works great!) Then, make the HUMMINGBIRD NECTAR on page 15.

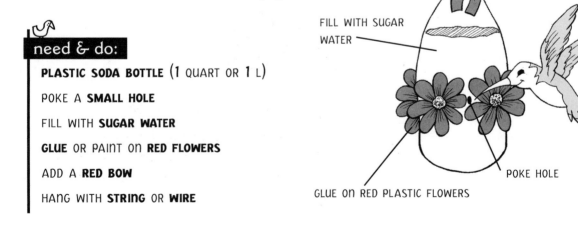

ADD RED BOW

FILL WITH SUGAR WATER

GLUE ON RED PLASTIC FLOWERS

POKE HOLE

need & do:

PLASTIC SODA BOTTLE (1 QUART OR 1 L)

POKE A **SMALL HOLE**

FILL WITH **SUGAR WATER**

GLUE OR PAINT ON **RED FLOWERS**

ADD A **RED BOW**

HANG WITH **STRING** OR **WIRE**

#8

Rockin' Robin Diner

Bring the birds in your neighborhood right to your window with a
birdseed bonanza. Make a pint-sized (500 ml) feeder for small birds or
a half-gallon (2 L) Rockin' Robin Diner for your larger feathered friends!

HANG WITH STRING

CUT CARTON

BIRDSEED

ADD A PERCH

need & do:

CUT **MILK CARTON** AS SHOWN

HANG WITH **HEAVY-DUTY STRING** OR **MONOFILAMENT**
   FISHING LINE

ADD A **STICK** OR **DOWEL** PERCH

FILL WITH **BIRDSEED**

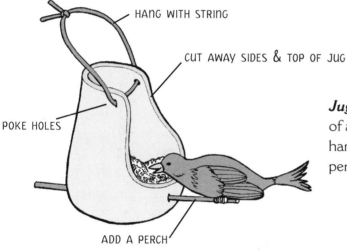

HANG WITH STRING

CUT AWAY SIDES & TOP OF JUG

POKE HOLES

ADD A PERCH

Jug Bird Feeder: Cut away the sides and top
of a plastic milk jug. Poke holes in the top to
hang; fill with seeds. You can even add a
perch if you like!

Quick Starts ꙮ Tips!™

Outsmart the squirrels

To squirrel-proof hanging feeders, try
using 3' to 4' (90 to 120 cm) of monofilament fishing line instead of wire or string.

Baffle Unwanted Guests!

Who else loves bird feed? Squirrels! Now there is nothing wrong with squirrels, except they can eat a whole feeder full of feed before a bird even gets a bite! You see, sharing is not one of a squirrel's finer qualities!

The Plan of Action

Let's take a three-part plan of action:

AVOID JUMPING-OFF POINTS! Squirrels are clever and agile, too — jumping as much as 10' (3 m) from the nearest leaping-off point (and they are happy to eat hanging upside down, too)!

BUILD A "FOIL 'EM" FEEDER. Feed the squirrels peanuts or dried ears of corn on their own feeder to keep them happy. Just be sure to locate it away from your bird feeders!

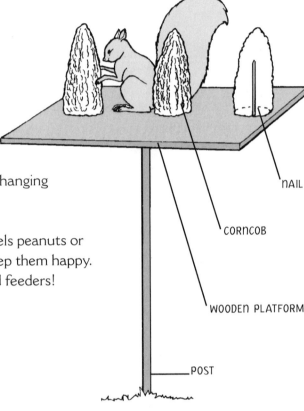

NAIL

CORNCOB

WOODEN PLATFORM

POST

PIE-TIN BAFFLE

BUILD A BAFFLE. To protect against food raids, add a baffle to your feeders. A baffle prevents the squirrel from getting close enough to the feeder to chow down on the feed. Attach the baffle below platform and covered feeders and above hanging feeders. Pie tins work well, but you can also use old record albums, large soda bottles, pieces of metal or stovepipe, or whatever works!

REAL ESTATE:

May We Show You Something in Bark?

Ah! Home, sweet home! We all know what makes our house into our home, and much of it has to do with our personal needs and preferences! Birds are the same way. For some birds, like robins and orioles, a simple nest in a tree or shrub is all they need. Others, like chickadees and bluebirds, will happily call a sturdy birdhouse home. Whether your bird real estate is simple or elaborate, chances are good there's a bird just waiting to move in!

To each her own!

Bird homes generally fall into two categories. Robins and phoebes are in the first group, the *platform nesters*. Since these popular songbirds are found just about everywhere in a variety of habitats (woodlands to inner-city parks to your backyard), you're likely to see some of their dwellings in your neighborhood! To help attract them, see NICE-'N'-NEW NESTS, below. You may be surprised at what these birds will choose for their "perfect" home: Someone we know has a robin build a nest every year on the flat wooden surface of some hanging wind chimes!

Birds that use birdhouses are called *cavity nesters*. No, they don't nest in your teeth, but they do like the confined, cozy space of a birdhouse or a hole in a tree. Bluebirds, nuthatches, woodpeckers, titmice, and wrens are just a few of the birds in this group. You may want to build some special dwellings for them. Try the SIMPLE GOURD HOUSE on page 39 or one of the fancier abodes on page 41–52.

Quick Starts™ No-Fuss Homesteads

To help the birds build their dream homes, supply nesting materials and simple shelters to suit their style.

Nice-'n'-New Nests

Attract birds that are building their nests in early spring for laying their eggs and raising their families by supplying an assortment of nest-building materials. Leave them where they can be easily spotted: Hang them in a mesh bag (the kind onions come in), decorate an evergreen tree with materials, or leave them in a basket in the middle of the lawn. A shallow pan filled with some wet dirt that will be used as the mortar will be appreciated, too!

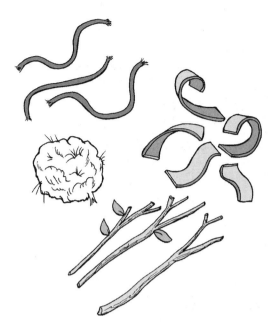

- dried grass and moss
- short pieces of string and yarn ("un-knit" an old sweater)
- stuffing from old furniture
- cotton balls
- dryer lint (save in a bag throughout the winter)
- wood shavings
- cellophane "grass" from Easter baskets
- short twigs
- fabric scraps, cut into small strips

Watch from the window to see birds helping themselves! Then, keep an eye out for familiar bits of material in bird nests around your yard. If you look very carefully, you may see several nests made with your help!

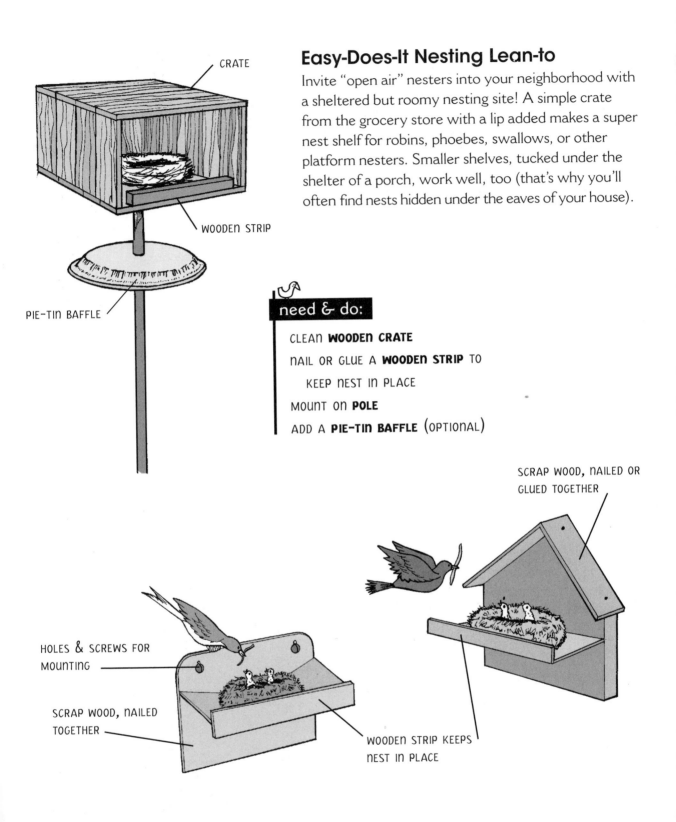

CRATE

WOODEN STRIP

PIE-TIN BAFFLE

Easy-Does-It Nesting Lean-to

Invite "open air" nesters into your neighborhood with a sheltered but roomy nesting site! A simple crate from the grocery store with a lip added makes a super nest shelf for robins, phoebes, swallows, or other platform nesters. Smaller shelves, tucked under the shelter of a porch, work well, too (that's why you'll often find nests hidden under the eaves of your house).

need & do:

CLEAN **WOODEN CRATE**

NAIL OR GLUE A **WOODEN STRIP** TO
    KEEP NEST IN PLACE

MOUNT ON **POLE**

ADD A **PIE-TIN BAFFLE** (OPTIONAL)

SCRAP WOOD, NAILED OR
GLUED TOGETHER

HOLES & SCREWS FOR
MOUNTING

SCRAP WOOD, NAILED
TOGETHER

WOODEN STRIP KEEPS
NEST IN PLACE

A Simple Gourd House

Natural gourds make great birdhouses, and they're easy to make and set up — no wood needed! The rounded gourd shape makes a perfect perch for the parents and nestlings, and the natural skin of the gourd provides good ventilation. Because the houses sway in the wind, they're less likely to be taken over by house sparrows and starlings or bothered by predators.

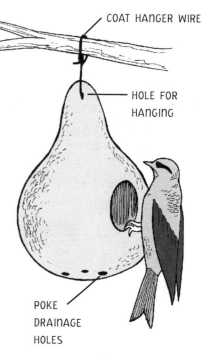

COAT HANGER WIRE

HOLE FOR HANGING

POKE DRAINAGE HOLES

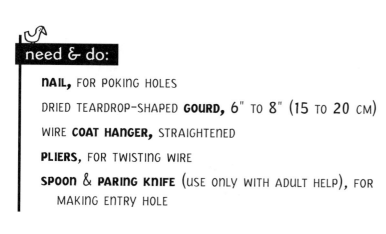

need & do:

NAIL, FOR POKING HOLES

DRIED TEARDROP-SHAPED **GOURD,** 6" TO 8" (15 TO 20 CM)

WIRE **COAT HANGER,** STRAIGHTENED

PLIERS, FOR TWISTING WIRE

SPOON & **PARING KNIFE** (USE ONLY WITH ADULT HELP), FOR MAKING ENTRY HOLE

1. Use a nail to poke a hole near the top of the gourd. Push the wire coat hanger through the hole and twist it into a loop for hanging.

2. Hollow out a rounded hole for the bird to enter (see the chart on page 60 for exact hole sizes for different birds) in the center of the gourd. Ask an adult to help puncture (or drill) through the gourd's tough outer skin. Shake out the dried seeds inside, and poke several 1/4" (5 mm) drain holes in the bottom.

3. Hang from a tree branch or a horizontal wire, and wait for your new neighbor to move in!

A Keep-Dry Canopy: Be sure to position the entrance hole in the center of the gourd: If it's too high up, water will drip in during rain. You may want to attach a little plastic or aluminum canopy over the doorway. Now that is quite posh!

The Martins Are Coming!

Gourd houses are great for small birds, and they've long been a favorite of purple martins, too! Purple martins like to nest in groups, so if you want to attract them, plan on making about eight gourd houses at once. Hang them close together, 6' to 20' (2 to 6 m) from the ground – purple martins like their houses high! – in an open area. Make the entrance holes 2¼" (5.5 cm) wide, and paint the outside of the house white to help reflect the heat.

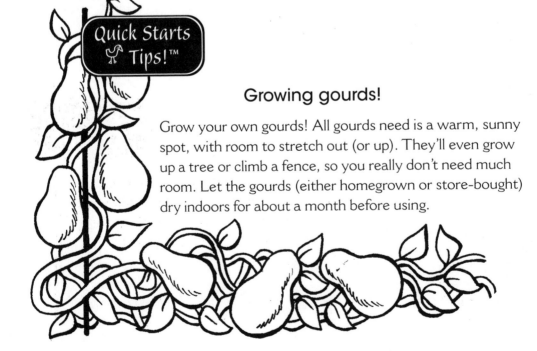

**Quick Starts
♁ Tips!™**

Growing gourds!

Grow your own gourds! All gourds need is a warm, sunny spot, with room to stretch out (or up). They'll even grow up a tree or climb a fence, so you really don't need much room. Let the gourds (either homegrown or store-bought) dry indoors for about a month before using.

Custom-Built Bird Housing!

irds returning to their summer habitats every year are faced with finding new homes, and many are finding it harder each year to find nesting sites in the wild. You can help out by building safe, cozy housing that meets their needs.

The custom houses that people make for birds are called nesting boxes and — just like your house — they can be various shapes and sizes. Choose a design to attract the birds in your area, and then make it yourself!

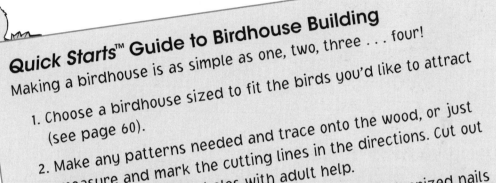

Quick Starts™ Guide to Birdhouse Building

Making a birdhouse is as simple as one, two, three . . . four!

1. Choose a birdhouse sized to fit the birds you'd like to attract (see page 60).

2. Make any patterns needed and trace onto the wood, or just measure and mark the cutting lines in the directions. Cut out the pieces and drill holes with adult help.

3. Assemble the birdhouse with a hammer and galvanized nails or a screwdriver and screws, and place it where the birds will find it (see Mix-'n'-Match!, page 58–59)!

4. Be sure the roof is hinged or easily unscrews so you can clean the house when the family moves out.

Quick Starts ❦ Tips!™

Extra-easy cutting

No saw or drill on hand? No problem! Many lumberyards or home-building supply stores will make all the cuts for you for a minimal fee — about 50¢ a cut. And you can still do all the assembly at home!

Open house

The best time to put up a new birdhouse is in late autumn. This not only gives the unpainted wood time to age, but the houses will be in place when the first birds return in spring. In the South, be sure all birdhouses are in place by late February, and in northern regions, get your birdhouses up by late March. Don't be discouraged if it takes awhile for the birds to find the nesting boxes — they'll come eventually!

Bird Design & Architecture Notes

Why wood? Wood "breathes" and will last for many seasons. It insulates, too, keeping out excess heat and cold. Cedar and cypress woods last the longest, but pine is probably the best choice for you to work with because it's inexpensive to buy and easy to hammer or drill into. A rough "face" or side on the inside of the birdhouse makes it easiest for birds to climb in and out, but even finished wood can be used if you scratch some footholds on the inside surface. Just be sure to avoid wood treated with stains or preservatives — the fumes from the chemicals could harm the birds.

Size to fit. Since cavity nesters range in size from a chickadee to a turkey vulture, there's no such thing as "one size fits all." Decide what type of bird you want to attract, and then build a nest box for that particular bird (see page 60 for entryway sizes and a website resource for variations of box size).

Color me natural. Cedar or cypress birdhouses don't need paint, but one made from pine might last longer with an outer coat of color. If you want to paint your bird-house, keep in mind that birds prefer dull, weathered grays and tans that reflect the sunlight and heat and are less obvious to predators. The birds will probably avoid a brightly painted house or one with a metal roof (hot and attracts predators). If you can find wood with the bark still on it, some birds like that best of all.

Use only water-based exterior latex paint, and *never paint or stain the inside of the box or the entrance hole* — the fumes given off can be toxic to the birds. Wait to install the box for at least two weeks after painting.

Quick Starts™ Slant-Top Songbird House

This birdhouse is measured and cut from pine lumber — no patterns required! It is a custom fit for bluebirds, and nuthatches, titmice, downy woodpeckers, chickadees, wrens, and other songbirds may be enticed to come if you vary the entrance hole dimension (see page 60).

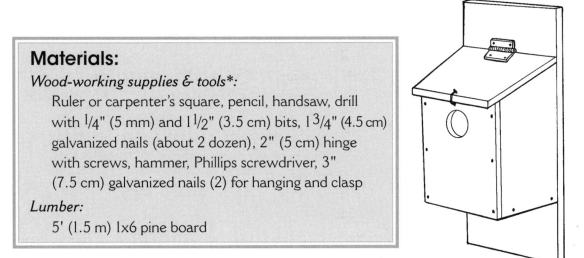

Materials:

Wood-working supplies & tools*:

Ruler or carpenter's square, pencil, handsaw, drill with $1/4$" (5 mm) and $1 1/2$" (3.5 cm) bits, $1 3/4$" (4.5 cm) galvanized nails (about 2 dozen), 2" (5 cm) hinge with screws, hammer, Phillips screwdriver, 3" (7.5 cm) galvanized nails (2) for hanging and clasp

Lumber:

5' (1.5 m) 1x6 pine board

*Note: You can build a lot of really cool things with tools, but handling them is serious business. Use only with adult supervision! And please, always return them to their proper storage space.

A word on wood

When you go to the lumberyard or home-building supply store to get your wood, you'll be asking for a "one by six" (1 x 6) pine board. But if you take it home and measure it, you'll find it's actually $3/4$" x 5 $1/2$" (2 x 13.5 cm). Wait — did it shrink on the way home? Lumber is sized according to its rough cut from the tree, before it's planed and sanded at the sawmill. So a 1" x 6" (2.5 x 15 cm) "rough" board becomes a slightly thinner and narrower finished board, which is just fine!

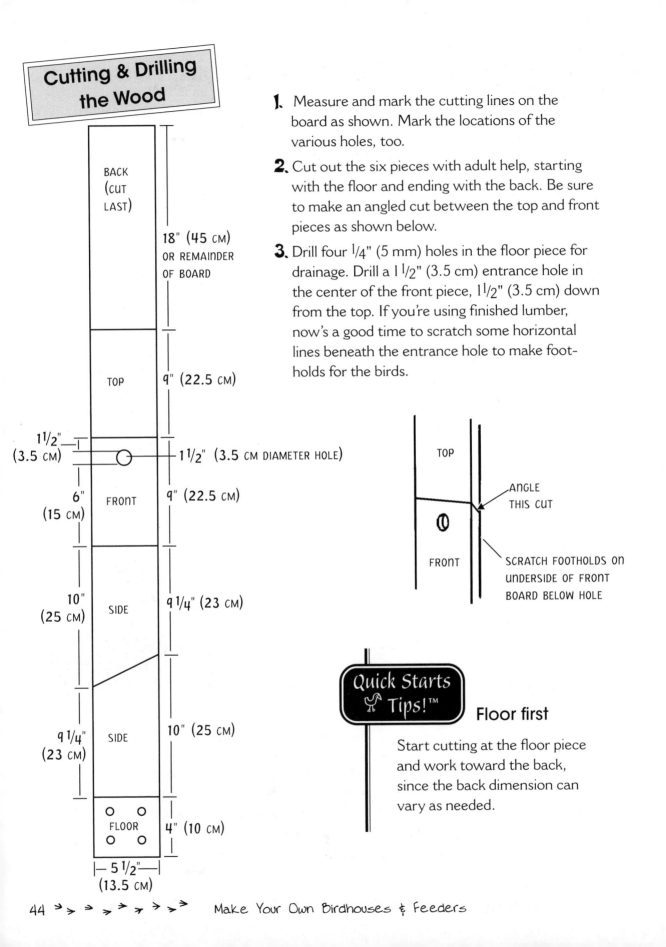

Cutting & Drilling the Wood

BACK
(CUT
LAST)

18" (45 CM)
OR REMAINDER
OF BOARD

TOP

9" (22.5 CM)

1½"
(3.5 CM)

1½" (3.5 CM DIAMETER HOLE)

6"
(15 CM)

FRONT

9" (22.5 CM)

10"
(25 CM)

SIDE

9¼" (23 CM)

9¼"
(23 CM)

SIDE

10" (25 CM)

FLOOR

4" (10 CM)

— 5½" —
(13.5 CM)

1. Measure and mark the cutting lines on the board as shown. Mark the locations of the various holes, too.

2. Cut out the six pieces with adult help, starting with the floor and ending with the back. Be sure to make an angled cut between the top and front pieces as shown below.

3. Drill four ¼" (5 mm) holes in the floor piece for drainage. Drill a 1½" (3.5 cm) entrance hole in the center of the front piece, 1½" (3.5 cm) down from the top. If you're using finished lumber, now's a good time to scratch some horizontal lines beneath the entrance hole to make footholds for the birds.

TOP

ANGLE
THIS CUT

FRONT

SCRATCH FOOTHOLDS On
UNDERSIDE OF FRONT
BOARD BELOW HOLE

Quick Starts Tips!™

Floor first

Start cutting at the floor piece and work toward the back, since the back dimension can vary as needed.

⇗ ⇗ ⇗ ⇗ ⇗ ⇗ ⇗   *Make Your Own Birdhouses & Feeders*

Assembling the Birdhouse

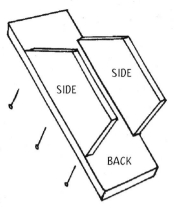

1. Center the side panels between the top and bottom edges of the back panel. Hammering from the back, use three nails to attach each side panel to the back panel.

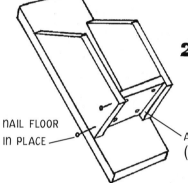

2. Slide the floor between the two sides, setting it 1/4" (5 mm) up from the bottom edge of the side pieces. Nail in place with two nails on each side.

NAIL FLOOR IN PLACE

ALLOW 1/4" (5 MM) RECESS

NAIL FRONT IN PLACE

(FOOTHOLDS INSIDE)

3. Attach the front panel on top of the side panels, flush to the side edges, with three nails on each side.

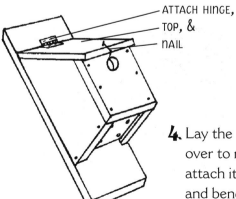

ATTACH HINGE, TOP, & NAIL

4. Lay the top in place (you'll need to turn the board over to make the angle fit with the back piece); attach it to the back with the hinge. Hammer in and bend up a large nail to secure the front shut.

5. Mark the center of the back panel just above the roof. Hammer a large nail through and mount your birdhouse on a sturdy post, 4' to 6' (1.25 to 1.75 m) off the ground.

Quick Starts ✍ Tips!™

Location, location, location

Birds, like humans, have preferences about location: Some like a house in an open field or at the edge of the woods. Some like them quite high, and others prefer lower locales. Check the preferred habitat for each bird on page 60, and then keep these tips in mind:

• Poles are better for mounting houses than trees, which are easily climbed by raccoons, cats, and squirrels.

• Place nest boxes away from noisy livestock, people, and streets.

• Hang the house away from dense shade. But in warm climates, place houses where they will receive some shading during the day so they won't overheat, and face entrance holes to the east or northeast.

• Don't put birdhouses next to feeders.

• Give each species some room: Bluebirds need about 300' (100 m) between pairs of boxes, and other birds need about 25' (7.75 m) between boxes. Put only one box in a tree.

• If your birdhouse is near a road, face it away from the traffic, so the fledglings won't fly into traffic.

Quick Starts™ Peaked Nesting Box

*W*elcome wrens to your yard with this perfectly peaked house! Or, by changing the entrance hole size and placement, you can attract chickadees, nuthatches, and other small songbirds. One side of the roof unscrews for easy cleaning in the spring.

Making the Patterns

1. Trace the patterns from pages 51–52 onto tracing paper. Cut out the tracing paper patterns, taping the patterns together as needed to make whole pieces.

2. Trace the paper patterns onto cardboard and cut out the cardboard pieces.

3. Label each piece with the pattern name and number of pieces to be cut. (You can also use the patterns to make a houselike feeder out of heavy-duty cardboard — see page 31.)

Materials:

Pattern-making supplies:
   Pencil, ruler, tracing paper, craft scissors, cardboard or heavy-duty paper

Wood-working supplies & tools*:
   Ruler or carpenter's square, pencil, handsaw, drill with ¼" (5 mm) and 1" (2.5 cm) bits, hammer, Phillips screwdriver, 1¾" (4.5 cm) galvanized nails, 1¼" (3 cm) galvanized drywall screws (2) for attaching the roof for easy cleaning, screw eye (optional)

Lumber:
   5' (1.5 m) 1x6 pine board

*Note: You can build a lot of really cool things with tools, but handling them is serious business. Use only with adult supervision! And please, always return them to their proper storage space.

Real Estate: May We Show You Something in Bark? ⟵ ⟵ ⟵ ⟵ ⟵ ⟵ ⟵ ⟵ ⟵ 47

Cutting & Drilling the Wood

1. Trace the patterns onto the wood. Mark all the holes.

2. Cut out the seven pieces with adult help. Drill the four 1/4" (5 mm) holes in the floor piece for drainage, and a 1" (2.5 cm) hole in the center of the front piece as shown on the pattern.

Assembling the Birdhouse

1. Lay the long edges of the side panels against the back panel. Use two nails to attach each side panel to the back panel.

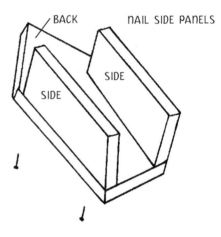

BACK

NAIL SIDE PANELS

SIDE

SIDE

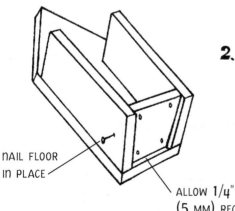

NAIL FLOOR IN PLACE

ALLOW 1/4"
(5 MM) RECESS

2. Slide the floor between the two sides, setting it 1/4" (5 mm) up from the bottom edge of the side pieces. Nail in place with one nail on each side.

Make Your Own Birdhouses & Feeders

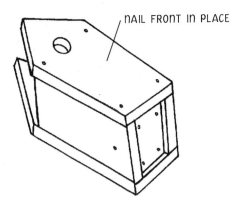

NAIL FRONT IN PLACE

3. Lay the front panel on top of the side panels so that the edges are flush. Hammer it in place with four nails as shown.

NAIL
SMALLER
ROOF PANEL

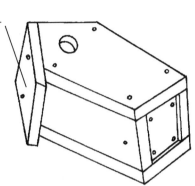

4. Lay the smaller roof panel (ROOF A) in place against the front and back panels, so that it's flush with the back and overhangs the front. Hammer it in place with two nails, one on each side.

SCREW LARGER ROOF
PANEL IN PLACE

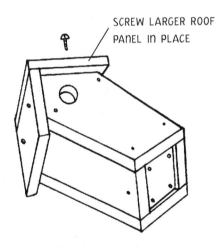

5. Place the larger roof panel (ROOF B) on the birdhouse, flush with the back panel and the other roof panel. Screw it in place with a screw on each side (it's easier if you predrill the holes).

Quick Starts ♫ Tips!™

Remember spring cleaning!

Always clean out all nest boxes each fall with soap and water, or between broods. If you leave your birdhouses out all winter, give them a thorough cleaning in early spring, in case winter birds (or other critters) used them for shelter.

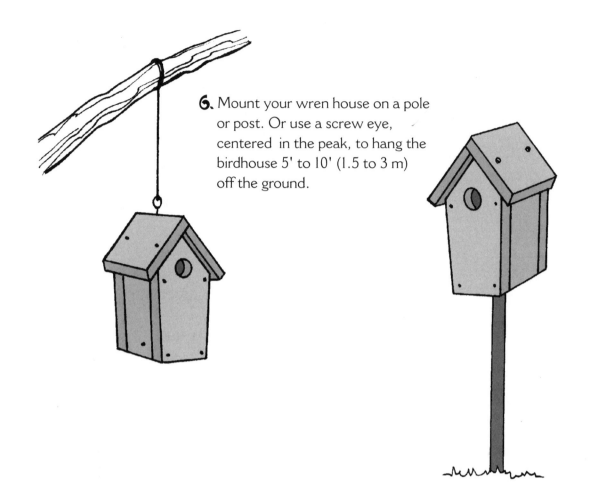

6. Mount your wren house on a pole or post. Or use a screw eye, centered in the peak, to hang the birdhouse 5' to 10' (1.5 to 3 m) off the ground.

Orphaned or Injured Birds

Sooner or later, you're bound to come across a baby bird out of its nest. What should you do? In most cases, leave the baby alone. Its parents are likely nearby, and they will attend to the bird. If the bird doesn't have its feathers yet, try to return it to its nest. Don't try to take it indoors or feed it — you will do more harm than good. And despite what you may have heard, don't worry that the parents will abandon the baby or the nest if you touch it. Birds actually have a very poor sense of smell.

If a bird hits your window and is not moving, leave it alone for 10 or 15 minutes to see if it recovers on its own. If it's obviously injured, call a local veterinarian for advice. *Don't try to give it first aid or food yourself.*

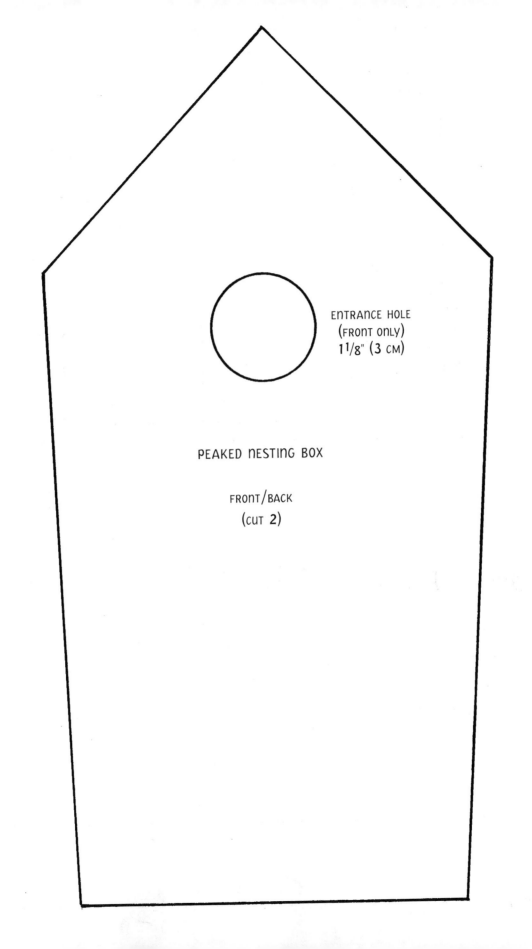

ENTRANCE HOLE
(FRONT ONLY)
$1^1/8$" (3 CM)

PEAKED NESTING BOX

FRONT/BACK
(CUT 2)

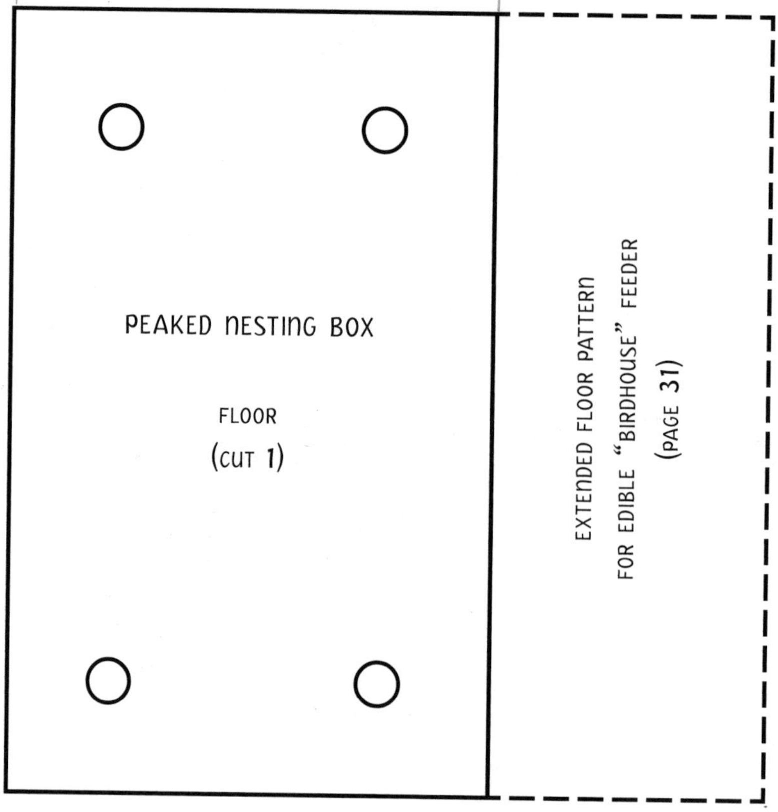

PEAKED NESTING BOX

FLOOR
(CUT 1)

EXTENDED FLOOR PATTERN
FOR EDIBLE "BIRDHOUSE" FEEDER
(PAGE 31)

ROOF B (CUT 1)

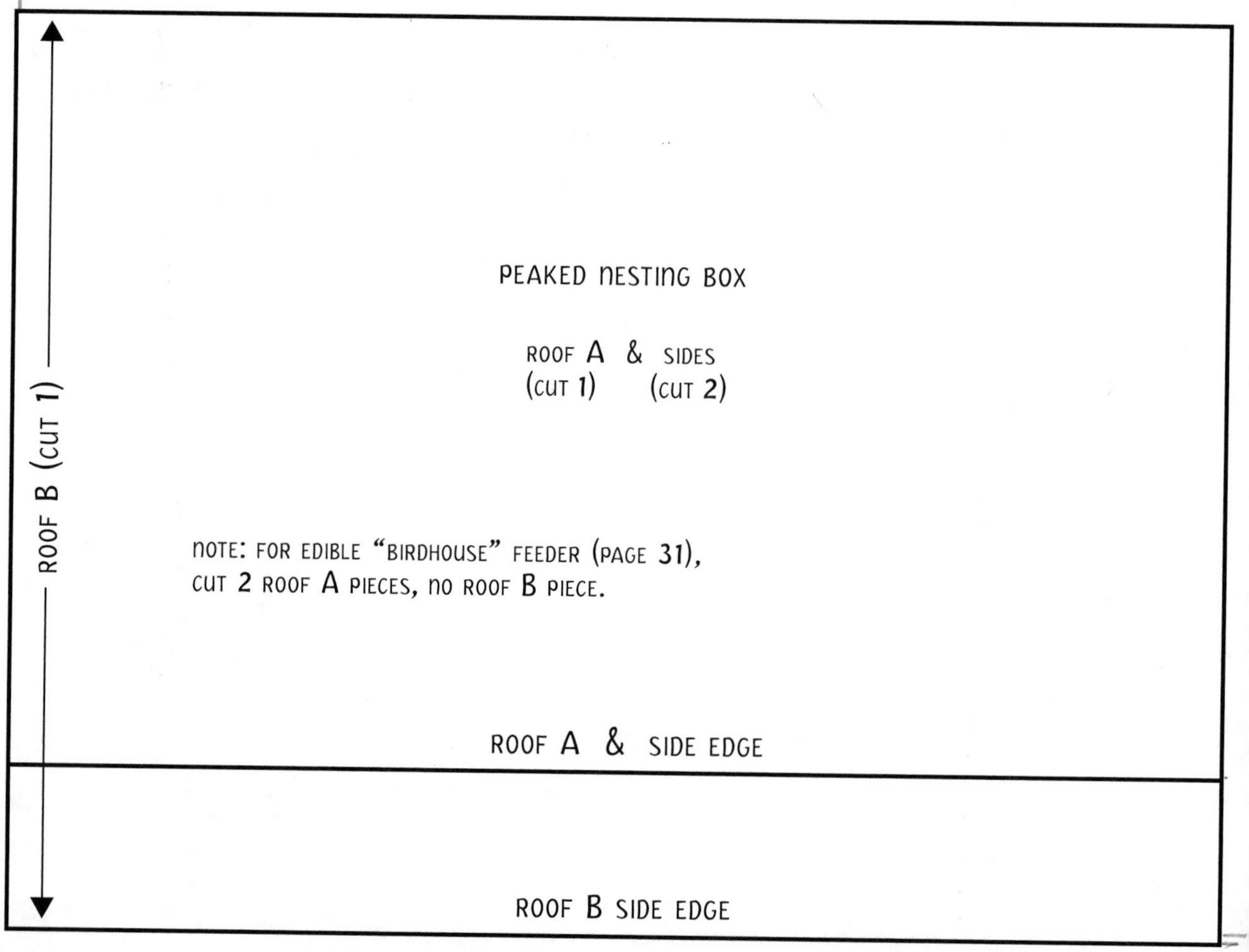

PEAKED NESTING BOX

ROOF A & SIDES
(CUT 1)   (CUT 2)

NOTE: FOR EDIBLE "BIRDHOUSE" FEEDER (PAGE 31),
CUT 2 ROOF A PIECES, NO ROOF B PIECE.

ROOF A & SIDE EDGE

ROOF B SIDE EDGE

WATER! WATER!

Splish Splash, I Was Taking a Bath!

Want to know one of the easiest ways to attract birds to your yard? Just provide some water for birds to drink and bathe in! Some birds will ignore feeders and houses, but will readily flock to your yard if you offer them a birdbath.

Water Safety for Birds

Keep it shallow. Birds that spend most of their time flying, such as swallows, dip into water while they're on the wing. But most birds prefer wading into very shallow water — no more than 2½" (6 cm) deep.

Elevate the bath. To keep bathing birds safe from cats and critters, raise the bath 2' to 3' (60 to 90 cm) above the ground, on a stump or an upside down flowerpot.

Make a beach. The best birdbaths slope to the deepest point so that birds can enter slowly, to a depth where they feel comfortable. Put sand in the bottom of the bath to give the birds sure footing, or place rocks along the way for perching.

Check the water, clean the tub. Change the water in your birdbath every couple of days to keep it fresh, and sponge out the bath once a week.

Quick Starts Tips!™

Birds, water & winter

If you're feeding birds in winter, check the water regularly to be sure it hasn't frozen over. Arrange a few branches or stones in the water in winter so that birds can stand on them and drink without getting wet. In summer, these "islands" will help waterlogged bugs, especially bees, climb to safety so they can fly away. (Never add antifreeze; it's poisonous to all animals, including birds and you.)

Quick Starts™ Birdbaths

Birds prefer firm footing, so if the bowl of your bath has a slick surface, add some sand to the bottom of it. Place your birdbath near a bush or tree where the birds can easily fly to safety to dry off (it's harder for them to fly when wet).

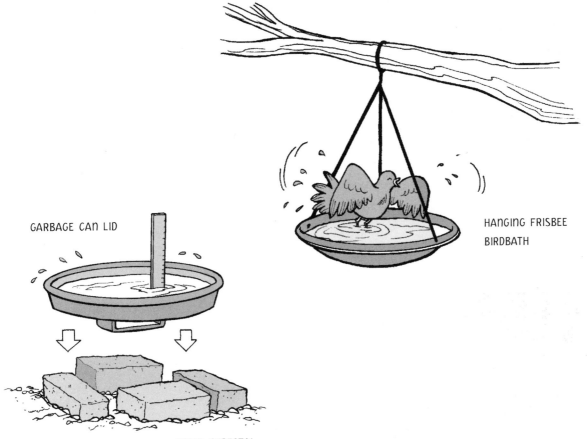

GARBAGE CAN LID

HANGING FRISBEE BIRDBATH

BRICK PEDESTAL

Quick Starts
🐦 Tips!™

A dripping fountain

Make a dripping fountain for your birdbath. Simply recycle an old bucket or plastic container by punching a tiny hole in the bottom, filling it with water, and hanging it above the birdbath so the water drips out very slowly. "Ah, delightful," say your guests!

SHALLOW PAN OR
HOLLOWED-OUT STUMP
FILLED WITH WATER

BAKING PAN MINIMUM SIZE:
9"x13"/22.5 x 32.5 CM
ON A FLAT RAILING, SECURED
WITH BUNGEE CORDS

PLANT SAUCER (AVAILABLE
AT PLANT NURSERIES) ATOP
PLASTIC MILK CRATE

Backyard Preserve Pool

Adding a pool to your property may sound like a major undertaking, but it's really very simple, if it's a miniature pool meant just for the birds!

1. Mark a shape you like on an areas that's roughly 2' x 3' (60 x 90 cm). Dig out a sloping hole from 1/2" (1 cm) to no more than 4" (10 cm) deep. (Remember, birds don't like deep water.)

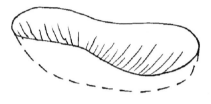

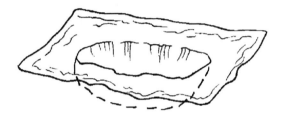

2. Cover with plastic (a double thickness of heavy-duty garbage bags).

3. Line the bottom of the hole with small smooth stones and cover edges with dirt.

4. Edge bird pool with decorative rocks. Add larger stone as perch. Fill with water.

MIX-'N'-MATCH!

Bird	Where It Lives	What It Eats	Types of Feeders
Blackbirds	different species throughout North America	sunflower seed, cracked corn, millet	tray, platform
Bluebirds	different species throughout North America	peanut butter, suet, fruit	tray, platform; suet feeder
Buntings	different species throughout U.S. & Canada	sunflower & thistle seeds, millet	platform
Cardinals	southwest, eastern, & central U.S., southern Canada	sunflower & safflower seeds, peanuts, peanut butter, fruit	hopper, tube, tray, platform; suet or peanut butter feeders
Cedar Waxwings	U.S. & Canada	sunflower seed, mealworms, fruit	platform
Chickadees	Carolina chickadee east to Texas; black capped chickadee throughout northern U.S. into Canada	sunflower, safflower, & thistle seeds, suet, peanuts	hanging, tube, tray or platform; thistle feeder; suet feeder or cakes
Doves & Pigeons	throughout U.S. & southern Canada	millet, milo, & thistle seeds, cracked corn, peanuts,	tray or platform
Finches	eastern & western U.S., southern Canada	sunflower, safflower, millet, & thistle seeds, peanuts, peanut butter, suet	hanging, tube or hopper, tray; thistle feeder; suet feeder or cakes
Flickers	throughout North America	suet or peanut butter	ground or tray; suet feeder or cakes; tree trunk
Grosbeaks	different species throughout U.S. & southern Canada	sunflower & safflower seeds	hanging, platform
Hummingbirds	northwestern & eastern U.S., Canada; some winter in Gulf states	sugar syrup	nectar feeder
Jays	blue jays east of the Rockies to southern Canada & Gulf of Mexico; other species mainly in western U.S. & Florida	sunflower & milo seeds, cracked corn, peanuts, suet, fruit	house or tube, tray or platform, suet feeder; tree trunk

Bird	Where It Lives	What It Eats	Types of Feeders
Juncos	throughout North America	sunflower, thistle & millet seeds, cracked corn, peanuts, peanut butter, suet	platform or tray; suet feeder or cakes; tree trunk
Kinglets	different species throughout North America	peanut butter, suet	suet feeder or cakes
Mockingbirds	southern Canada south to the Caribbean	fruit, suet or peanut butter	tray or platform; suet feeder
Nuthatches	different species throughout North America	sunflower & safflower seeds, suet, peanut butter	platform or tube; suet feeder or cakes
Orioles	summer throughout U.S. & southern Canada; winter in Mexico & southern U.S.	fresh fruit, grape jelly, sugar syrup, suet, nuts	hanging, tray or platform; nectar feeder
Robins	throughout North America	corn, dried & fresh fruits, nuts, peanut butter, suet	platform, hopper
Sparrows	throughout North America	sunflower & thistle seeds, cracked corn, millet, peanuts	hanging house or tube, tray or platform, thistle feeder
Tanagers	different species throughout U.S. & Canada	fruit, sugar syrup, suet	tray or platform; nectar feeder; suet feeder
Thrashers	different species throughout U.S. & southern Canada	fruit, cracked corn, nuts, peanut butter	hanging; suet feeder or cakes
Thrushes	different species throughout North America	peanut butter, suet, fruit, sugar syrup	hanging, nectar feeder
Titmice	different species in central & eastern U.S. & southwest Texas	sunflower & safflower seeds, peanuts, suet	tube, tray or platform; hanging suet feeder
Woodpeckers	different species throughout North America	sunflower seeds, peanuts, fruit, sugar syrup, suet, peanut butter	hanging, tube, platform, tree trunks; suet feeder or cakes; nectar feeder
Wrens	different species throughout U.S. & southern Canada	suet, peanut butter	hanging suet feeder or cakes

Canadian Province Birds & Canadian Territory Birds

Canadian Province Birds

Alberta: Great Horned Owl
British Columbia: Steller's Jay
Manitoba: Great Gray Owl
New Brunswick: Black-Capped Chickadee
Newfoundland: Atlantic Puffin & Willow Ptarmigan
Nova Scotia: Osprey
Ontario: Common Loon
Prince Edward Island: Blue Jay
Quebec: Snowy Owl
Saskatchewan: Sharp-Tailed Grouse

Canadian Territory Birds

Northwest Territories: Gyrfalcon
Nunavet: Rock Ptarmigan
Yukon: Common Raven

Quick Starts™ Guide to
Nesting-Box Entryway Sizes & Box Placement

A basic slant-top birdhouse or peaked-roof design will appeal to a number of different bird species. Just alter the size of the entrance hole to fit the bird. Then place the house where the birds prefer to live and wait for your new neighbors to arrive!

Bird	Entrance Hole Size	Box Distance from Ground	Preferred Placement
Bluebird	1 1/2" (3.5 cm)	4'–6' (1.25–1.75 m)	Open areas, fields; mountain and western bluebirds also like forest edges; face entrance northeast toward open area
Carolina Wren	1 1/2" (3.5 cm)	5'–10' (1.5–3 m)	Edge of woods; backyard
Cedar Waxwings			Nest in trees in open woodlands, orchards, backyards, and parks
Chickadee	1 1/8" (2.75 cm)	4'–15' (1.25–4.5 m)	Edge of woods, backyards; put 1" (2.5 cm) of wood shavings in box
Downy Woodpecker	1 1/4" (3 cm)	6'–20' (1.75–6 m)	Edge of woods
Northern Flicker**	2 1/2" (6 cm)	6'–20' (1.75–6 m)	Fields, groves, edge of woods; fill box with wood
Flycatcher**			
Great crested	1 3/4" (4.5 cm)	5'–15' (1.5–4.5 m)	Edge of woods, orchards, parks
Ash-throated	1 1/2" (3.5 cm)	5'–15' (1.5–4.5 m)	Dry plains, deserts, thickets, woodlands
House Wren	1–1 1/8" (2.5–3 cm)	5'–10' (1.5–3 m)	Edge of woods, backyard, near buildings
Nuthatch			
White-breasted	1 3/8" (3.25 cm)	5'–15' (1.5–4.5 m)	Edge of woods; add 1" (2.5 cm) of wood shavings
Red-breasted	1 1/4" (3 cm)	5'–15' (1.5–4.5 m)	Parks, shrubby areas, forests; add 1" (2.5 cm) of wood shavings
Phoebe*	—	8'–12' (2.5–3.75 m)	Backyards, near buildings, under bridges
Prothonotary warbler	1 1/8" (2.75 cm)	4'-8' (1.25–2.5 m)	Near or over water
Purple Martin	2 1/4" (5.5 cm)	6'-20' (1.75–6 m)	Open areas; no trees or buildings within 40' (12 m); paint house white
Robin*	—	6'–15' (1.75–4.5 m)	Buildings, trees, shrubs
Titmouse	1 1/4" (3 cm)	5'–15' (1.5–4.5 m)	Edge of woods; face hole away from wind
Tree Swallow	1 1/2" (3.5 cm)	5'–15' (1.5–4.5 m)	Open areas, fields, marshes; east facing

* Use a nesting shelf with an open front.
** These birds need slightly larger nesting boxes.

Careful measuring

Be precise on the entrance hole size. Bluebirds, for example, will nest in a box with a 1 1/2" (3.5 cm) hole, or an oval hole that measures 1 3/8" (3.25 cm) across and 2 1/4" (5.5 cm) high. But, a wider hole will allow starlings to evict the bluebirds. The same is true with chickadees and wrens — if the hole is larger than 1 1/8" (2.75 cm), house sparrows will probably move into the box instead!

U.S. State Birds
Find Your State Bird!

Alabama: Yellowhammer

Alaska: Willow Ptarmigan

Arizona: Cactus Wren

Arkansas: Mockingbird

California: California Valley Quail

Colorado: Lark Bunting

Connecticut: Robin

Delaware: Blue Hen Chicken

Florida: Mockingbird

Georgia Brown: Thrasher

Hawaii: Nene

Idaho: Mountain Bluebird

Illinois: Cardinal

Indiana: Cardinal

Iowa: Eastern Goldfinch

Kansas: Western Meadowlark

Kentucky: Cardinal

Louisiana: Eastern Brown Pelican

Maine: Chickadee

Maryland Baltimore: Oriole

Massachusetts: Chickadee

Michigan: Robin

Minnesota: Common Loon

Mississippi: Mockingbird

Missouri: Bluebird

Montana: Western Meadowlark

Nebraska: Western Meadowlark

Nevada: Mountain Bluebird

New Hampshire: Purple Finch

New Jersey: Eastern Goldfinch

New Mexico: Roadrunner

New York: Bluebird

North Carolina: Cardinal

North Dakota: Western Meadowlark

Ohio: Cardinal

Oklahoma: Scissor-Tailed Flycatcher

Oregon: Western Meadowlark

Pennsylvania: Ruffed Grouse

Rhode Island: Rhode Island Red

South Carolina: Great Carolina Wren

South Dakota: Ring-Necked Pheasant

Tennessee: Mockingbird

Texas: Mockingbird

Utah: American Seagull

Vermont: Hermit Thrush

Virginia: Cardinal

Washington: Willow Goldfinch

West Virginia: Cardinal

Wisconsin: Robin

Wyoming: Western Meadowlark

More Good Books from
WILLIAMSON PUBLISHING

Please see below for ordering information or to visit our website. Thank you.

The following *Quick Starts for Kids!*™ books for ages 8 to adult are each 64 pages, fully illustrated, trade paper, 8 x 10, $7.95 US.

BAKE THE BEST-EVER COOKIES!
by Sarah A. Williamson

•

BE A CLOWN!
Techniques From a Real Clown
by Ron Burgess

KIDS' EASY KNITTING PROJECTS
by Peg Blanchette

KIDS' EASY QUILTING PROJECTS
by Terri Thibault

•

MAKE YOUR OWN FUN PICTURE FRAMES!
by Matt Phillips

•

MAKE YOUR OWN HAIRWEAR!
Beaded Barrettes, Clips, Dangles & Headbands
by Diane Baker

MAKE YOUR OWN TEDDY BEARS & BEAR CLOTHES
by Sue Mahren

•

YO-YO!
Tips & Tricks From a Pro
by Ron Burgess

To see what's new at Williamson, visit our website at:

www.williamsonbooks.com

More Williamson Books for Kids!

Parents' Choice Approved
Parent's Guide Children's Media Award
BOREDOM BUSTERS!
The Curious Kids' Activity Book
by Avery Hart and Paul Mantell, $12.95

American Bookseller Pick of the Lists
Oppenheim Toy Portfolio Best Book Award
Parents' Choice Approved
SUMMER FUN!
60 Activities for a Kid-Perfect Summer
by Susan Williamson, $12.95

Parents' Choice Approved
KIDS' ART•WORKS!
Creating with Color, Design, Texture & More
by Sandi Henry, $12.95

Parents' Choice Gold Award
Dr. Toy Best Vacation Product
THE KIDS' NATURE BOOK
365 Indoor/Outdoor Activities & Experiences
by Susan Milord, $12.95

Prices may be slightly higher when purchased in Canada.

TO ORDER BOOKS:

We accept Visa and MasterCard *with number and expiration date.*
Toll-free phone orders with credit cards:

1-800-234-8791

Or, send a check with your order to:

Williamson Publishing Company
P.O. Box 185 Charlotte, VT 05445

Catalog request: mail, phone, or e-mail
info@williamsonbooks.com

Please add $4.00 for postage for one book plus $1.00 for each additional book. Satisfaction is guaranteed or full refund without questions or quibbles.